IRISH
SHOPFRONTS

**Introduction by
Patrick O'Donovan**

IRISH
SHOPFRONTS

**Photographs by
John Murphy**

St. Martin's Press ● *New York*

First published in the USA 1981 by
St Martin's Press, Inc.
175 Fifth Avenue
New York
NY 10010

ISBN 0-312-43623-8
Library of Congress Catalog Card Number: 80-52870

Published in Northern Ireland 1981 by
The Appletree Press Ltd

Typeset and designed in N. Ireland
Color separations by Graphic Reproductions (Dublin)
Printed in Singapore

Nations have many sorts of treasure. They have gold in cathedral treasuries, paintings in long galleries, great useless mansions that are yet the boast of their century. Such treasures, unless they be utterly private, are part of the wealth of ordinary life. And among the treasures that belong to a people, that add to the joy of living, that grow more marvellous the more you study them, are the shopfronts of Ireland.

The visitor is apt to be astonished by what he finds in Ireland. The place is marvellously alien. It talks, drinks, eats, behaves and looks different. True, the suburbs and new buildings are as boring as those of Leeds, Lyon, or Los Angeles. But in almost every town there is also a blaze of color which comes from the Irish themselves going wild. While Paris, London and Rome are splendidly grey, there begins a frivolity in Dublin born of color. The great town houses are pink. The pubs are fancifully painted—both as an invitation to alcoholic delight and as an alternative to what the Upper Crust would command. Indeed color may have been a form of rebellion through which the people's palaces, though they could not be built of granite or marble, could yet be as brilliant as theatre backdrops, gaily attesting to all the carelessly understood styles of Europe. And

Introduction by Patrick O'Donovan

her shopfronts are a very special expression of this repressed ebullience as well as their love of color, a taste never attributed to the Irish by the outside world.

In Ireland the villages were not the places where the people lived, but where they came for supplies and, most regularly, to attend church. Yet the shops did almost everything that the church could not do, and offered a flamboyant alternative, perhaps, to the latter's solemnity. The pub-shop, for instance, is peculiar to Ireland. Who could order a glass of *beaujolais* from among the sensible village shops of France? And you would get a most peculiar look if you asked for a pint of beer at a back counter in a small town drapers in England.

The village shop in Ireland with its small turnover, run by the Irish for the Irish, was originally a work place where there might be an enlarged window so that a cobbler or weaver could have better light for his work. Then when shops meant selling what other men made, there were furiously individual attempts to provide a facade that would attract a customer. When plate glass came to Ireland in the middle of the nineteenth century, the great sheets of glass tended to be divided up by pillars. Thus if a window got broken on a market day, not all of it went.

The result of this development and the influence of European styles of the time—classical, Gothic and *art nouveaux*—was a brilliant explosion of domestic architecture so typically and recognizably Irish that it is rightly called vernacular. Why it should have happened is not so easy to explain. A shopkeeping class asserting itself against the Ascendency? A love of color hitherto repressed by proverty? An act of enchanting snobbery, or some vast, private national joke? An assertion of gentility, or a talent too long hidden by others in its native ground? On this we can do little more than speculate. Perhaps the ultimate purpose of these shopfronts is the *fascia* or entablature that bears the name of the proprietor. All the small columns and glass rise to hold this horizontal board the whole length of the facade, and upon this the native imagination has run a small but gorgeous riot. Thus, above Irish shopfronts, you see names in a hundred different forms. There is cursive Victorian, *art nouveaux*, classical, celtic revival, solid great capital letters, and there is vulgarity raised to an art form, with gold and carving and all the brash colors of a healthy spectrum. All these are part of Ireland's unbroken tradition. They are unique, and will begin to be treasured when it is too late to save them. That happens everywhere with such objects. Yet these are not the crude by-products of some primitive or derivative art. They are part of a national culture that was denied its proper expression in other visual forms. Each one should be a joy to any observer.

McSwiggan's bar c. 1910 *(P.R.O.N.I.)* from
Brian Walker, *Shadows on Glass* (1976)

Contents

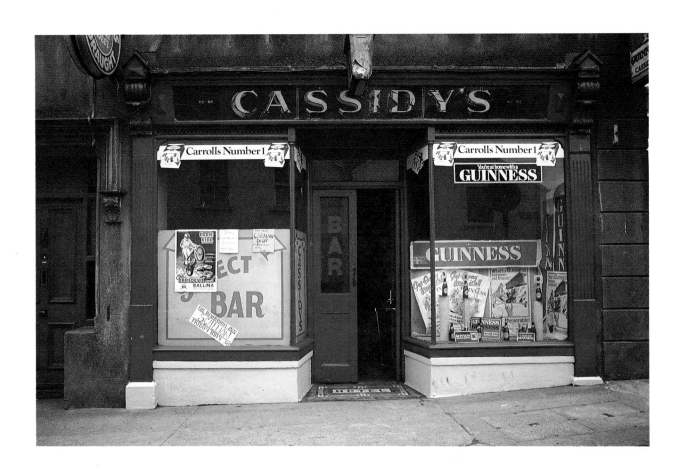

8

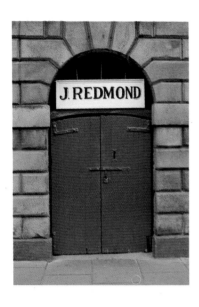

29

32

39

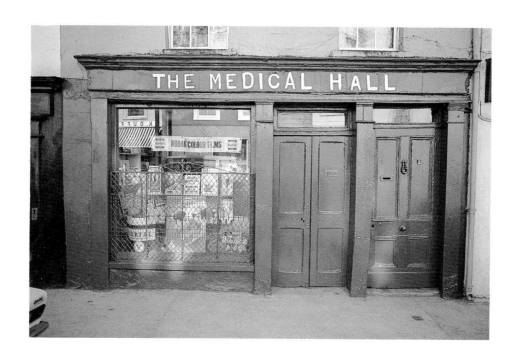

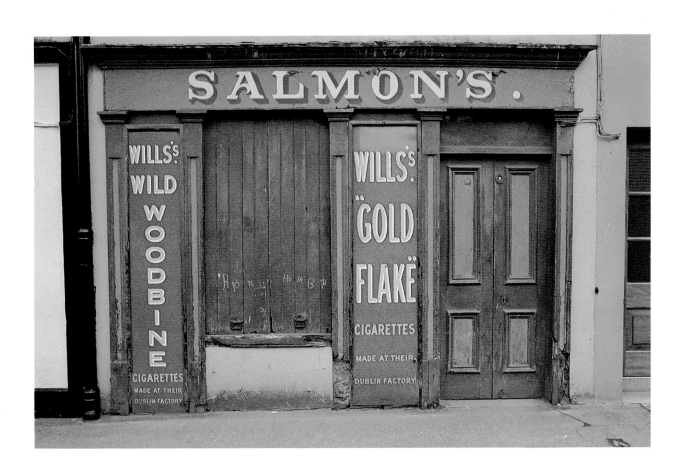

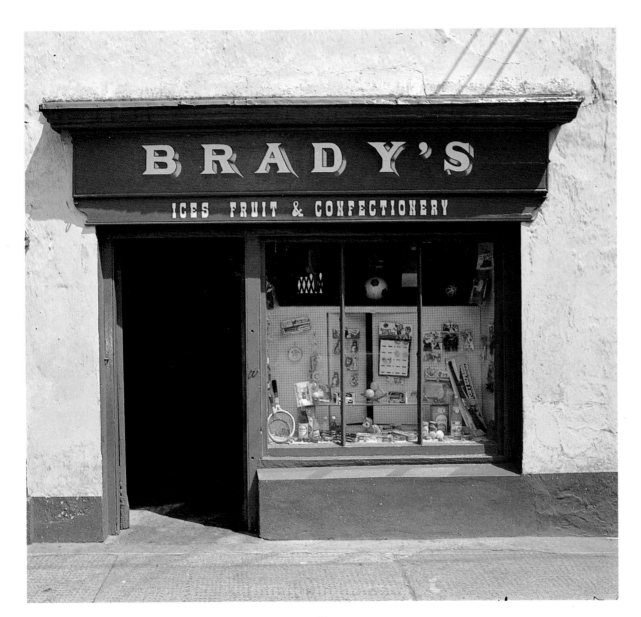

58

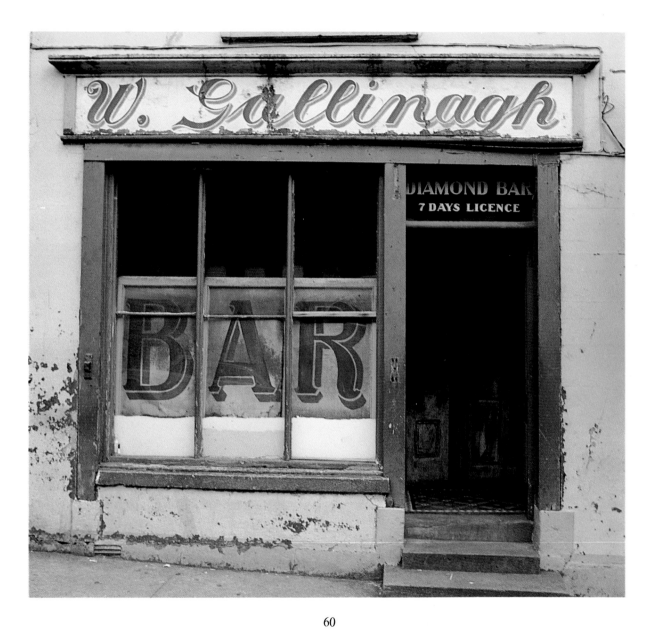

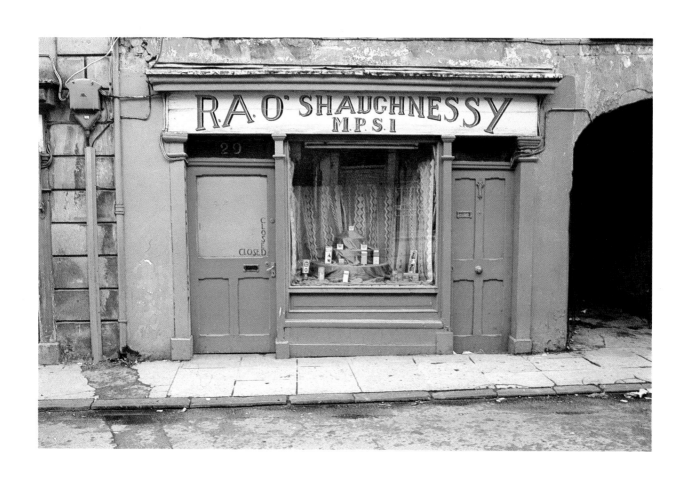

72

76

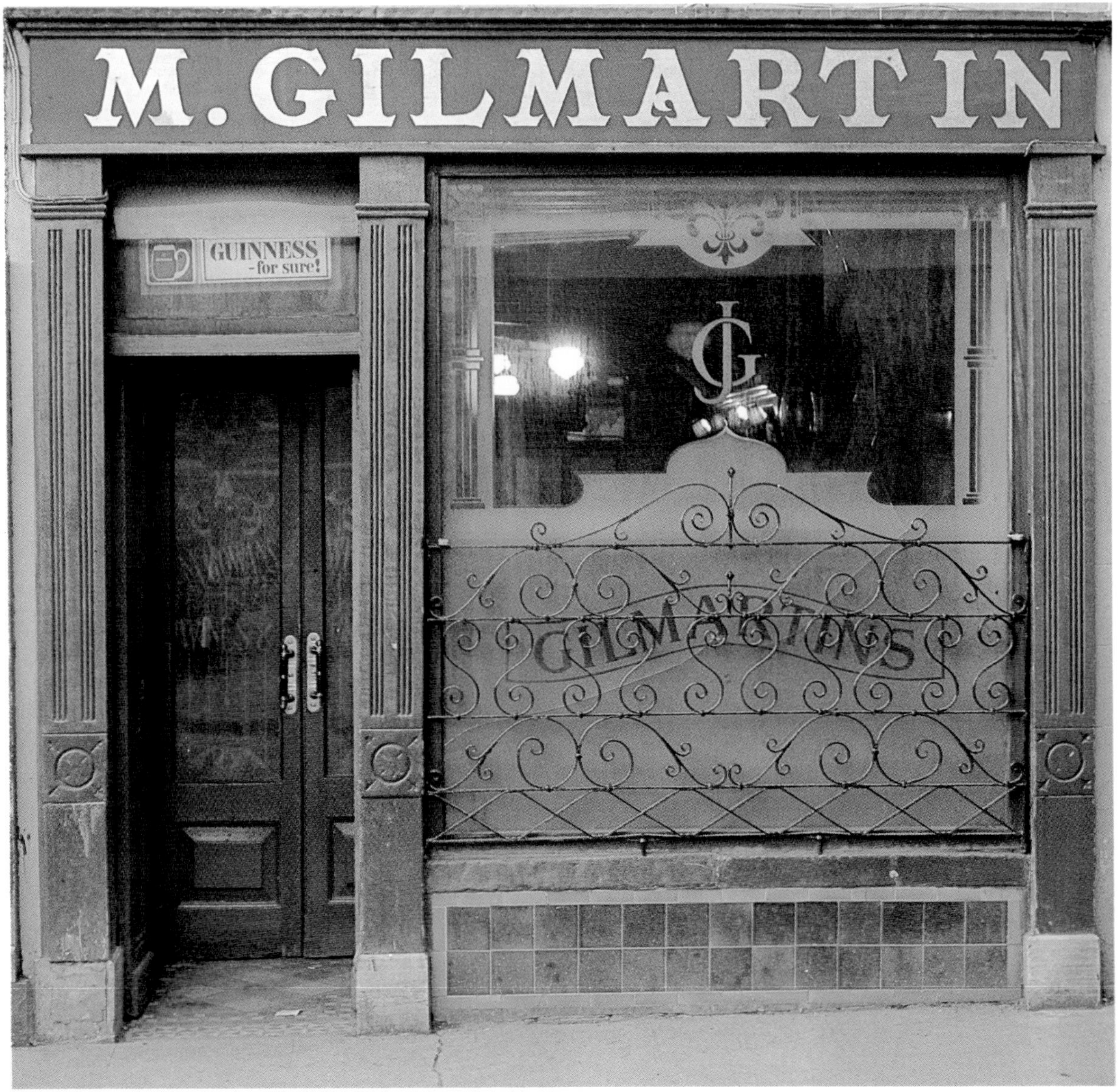
M. GILMARTIN
GUINNESS
-for sure!
GILMARTINS

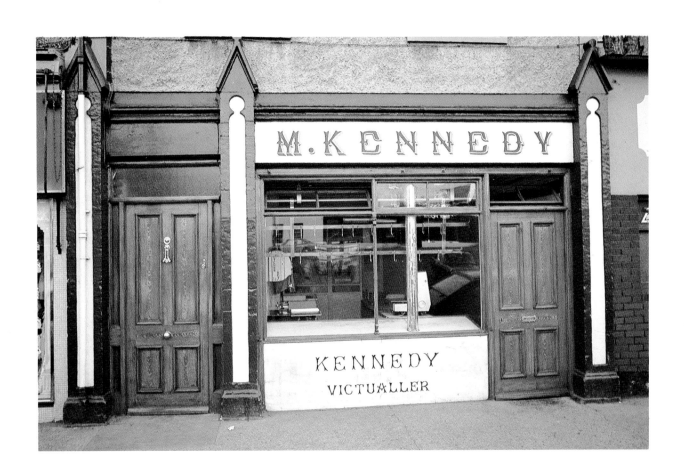

84

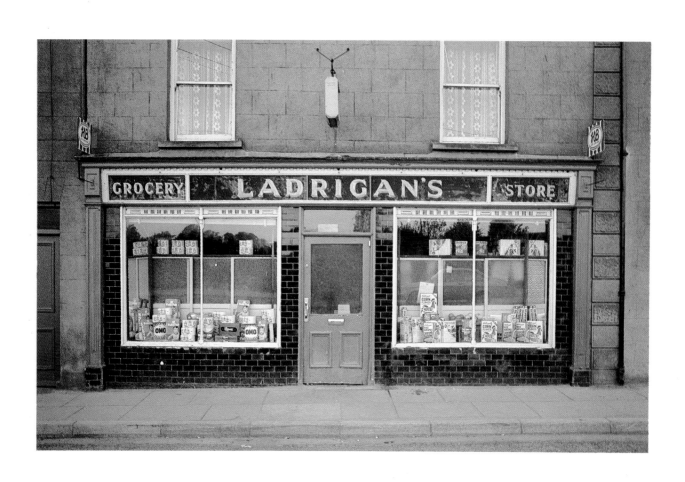

88

93

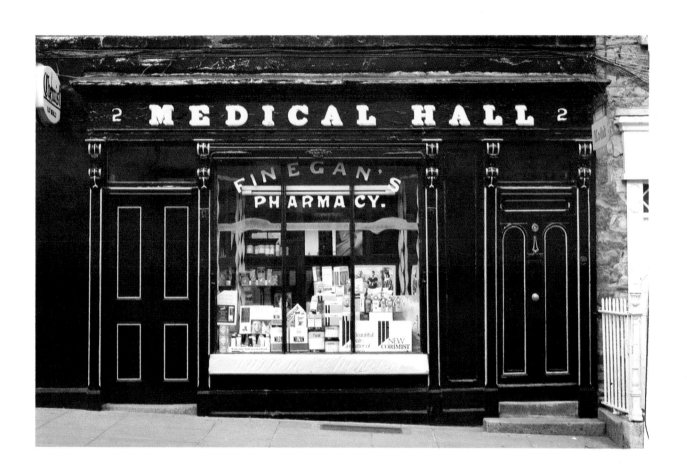